Abacus

Mary Karr

Abacus

Carnegie Mellon University Press
Pittsburgh 2007

Some of the poems in this book appeared originally in *Antioch Review, Columbia: A Magazine of Poetry & Prose, Crazyhorse, Cutbank, Ironwood, Mother Jones, Ploughshares, Poetry Northwest, Seneca Review, Sonora Review, 25 Minnesota Poets #2, Yankee.* "The Magnifying Mirror," "Hard Knocks," "Vigil," "For My Children," "Lipstick," "The Last Paris Poem," "Diogenes Tries to Forget," "My New Diet," "The Distance," "Witnessing My Father's Will," "Diogenes the Bartender Closes Up," "Diogenes Passes the Time," "Predictions," "Report," and "Diogenes Invents a Game" appeared originally in *Poetry.* "Insomnia" appeared in *Aspen Anthology.*

I owe special thanks to the National Endowment for the Arts, the Minnesota State Arts Board, and the MacDowell Colony, for time and money; and to Stephen Dobyns, Ellen Bryant Voigt, Bill Knott, Heather McHugh, Robert Long, and John Engman for help in editing individual poems, and to Michael Milburn for attention to the entire manuscript.

Abacus was first published by Wesleyan University Press in 1987.

The publisher wishes to acknowledge James Reiss and James W. Hall for their generous contributions to the Classic Contemporaries Series.

For Pete, Charlie, and Lecia
and for Michael

Contents

1

The Magnifying Mirror

I found it in my mother's purse: my face
in a blurred circle, upside down,
then my eye grew silver-dollar sized,
skin moon-cratered even then
though I ignored the velvet hairs
and precancerous moles I'd later call
my family traits. I was too young to hate

myself, just thrilled to be so big.
Later I shrank to see that face,
paid a psychiatrist 5000 bucks
to puff me up again. She shook her head.
She said I sounded like a lovely child
when I described my petty thefts, the shock
with which I stole my mother's face,
growing into her high heels,
her taste for alcohol and men.

This terrifies me so I keep a mirror in my purse,
take it out when I'm alone. Holding it arm's length
I re-create my nose dive from womb to earth.
Or I bring it close: beauty,
ugliness, who knows how many times
each flaw and fear can be magnified,
or whether birth is something to overcome
gradually, not by looking out,
but by looking in.

Diogenes Invents a Game

My latest hobby deals with dark,
   that inky sea I occupy.
Some nights supine for hours, I pluck
   a mattress button, flip it,
hear it fall. I divide the world
   into increasingly small
squares to reach that echoed spot
   until last night the button
didn't land. I found it in a spider's web
   at dawn. So much
for calculus. The bug looked
   equally confused,
having worked like a wild violinist
   for its worthless bundle
of thread. It touched its head
   in poisonous salute
before returning to its sticky
   jigsaw, that little
fence against the war with dark.

(for John Engman)

4

A Ballet in Numbers for Mary Ellen

Whatever I was too stupid to learn, you knew by heart:
French, where to put rhinestones.
How to print the numbers in calculus to resemble
a ballet troupe at the barre. Wild,
but well behaved. That's how we were photographed
as girls, textbooks open, dreaming of swans.

But those aren't swans that glide down the corridor,
just nurses who're white and mean
to do you harm, their pockets full of matches, razors,
their tablets guaranteed to make you beautiful.
Lately, you swallow everything,
and you don't think you're a genius any more.
Or so you tell me on the phone, having noticed
a chaos in the lines of the dictionary,
in your husband's signature on the divorce papers—
the "t" slashed in half, the "i" dotted
with an ice pick. The last word in your explanation
is *ennui*, correctly spoken, from long habit.

The doctors inject their formulas promising
grace. Well, that's bunk.
Lots of things just don't add up,
and you're left coloring the zeroes red in the margins.
Or on tiptoes before the final text
of the mirror, fanning out your pink nightgown,
holding up empty arms.

If you're creating a new language,
send me the grammar, a few key phrases.
Or if you're walking down a ruler, notice the distance

between zero and one: as the units get smaller
you approach the truth. So let's go back
to *The History of Ballet*; the prima ballerina sprawled
into an X on page 92, by 93 has left the frame.
Every leap is a leap of faith, and those roses
waiting in the wings have their perfume. Still,
beauty occurs in midair, when the dancer's face
is clenched with fear. Or in the clumsy way
people put their hands together,
the little marks they make on paper.
Where does the accent go in *mon ami*?

Taking Out the Lawn Chairs

When I wake with the first snails of sweat
   on my upper lip,
I know the Perrys will be taking down the lawn chairs.
Betty, her lap full of needlepoint, will store
a bushel of peas on the back porch, for later, for company.
Jim stands before a refrigerator full of beer,
his red cap over the crease in his brow;
he tucks a plug of tobacco inside his lower lip
and keeps the coffee can beside his chair.
All summer it will last just this way—
the grandchildren corralled into hats and rubber thongs,
and still, the bee stings, the red storm of freckles.

The pecans harden to pebbles and drop to the ground
in the first big rain of November,
and before there is time even to make a pie
we are putting away the lawn chairs.
All the chrome joints are rusted stiff, and their squeak
startles the gray cat under the house.
The bonnets droop from nails in the garage,
and Jim is saying, Hardly worth the trouble.
His head shakes like a blue tick hound's
as he strains to lug chairs to the basement.
It's the smallest of deaths that is most telling.
He's too tired to rake the leaves this year
though he's knee deep in them,
and the ocean wind tears them
and pecans hail to the ground.
The even rows of chairs, stoic in the damp cellar,
keep him satisfied on the dark stairs
thinking only of the sheets folded back on his bed
(those resting arms) distant and inviting as winter.

Aunt Gladys

You took a basket, filled it with berries.
You took them home to make a purple pie
that stained my mouth and your hands,
but I was never part of your nest. I went barefoot,
wouldn't wear a bonnet and was always freckled.
I couldn't cook huge white biscuits
or pies that bled beautifully onto the pan.

You can't see me when I enter the room.
You've cooked too much. I'm embarrassed
to introduce another lover. This time my skin
is pale as paper. My voice has lost its rhythm.
I smoke too much. My clothes are from the city,
and you say I look like a Christmas ornament,
gaudy and useful for only one day.
Uncle Ott has become simple.
He says only "Howdy doo."
I say it's a thing called aphasia,
but you know he's folding up
like a mimosa tree at sundown.
You want to show me the cows, the grandkids,
the house on the river, the indoor bathroom.
I want to see you alone in your barnboard kitchen.

Now I'm ready for your nest.
I've been out, and you've waited—
a great owl, a small hole in dark wood.
I want suddenly to be rolled
into your crockery bowl,
and left on the warm oven,
with a damp towel over me, to rise.

The Lynched Man

It was not my first death. I had coiled
the rare wood and fabric of stiff kittens
into a shoe box, toyed with the blood-dried stumps
of squirrel tails after the hunt.

I knew vertigo, large hands lowering me
into a casket to kiss a grandparent's waxy cheek,
the hot wind of palm-leaf funeral fans: on one side
a prayer, on the other a day-glo Jesus

shining in a Louisiana sunset. But the lynched man
missed a shoe. He twirled like a tire swing
in the breeze that stirred the sugar cane, which made
a clacking noise like primitive instruments.

I hooked my finger in my uncle's belt loop
and stared, idly wondering who owned the white
cotton shirt shrouding the corpse's face.
My uncle's fragrance of cows and tobacco

was a cloud I hoped would envelop me
while he opened his pocket knife,
instructing me to wait.
That smell swamped my memory tonight

when I stepped eye level into a giant bat,
which clung to a branch with curled claws.
Its leafy wings cloaked its head,
furred and mysterious. I felt the urge

to kill, hurled a stone so it dropped
in my path. Little neck-snapped rodent,
little cruelty surge that spread
like an ivory flag unfurling in my chest.

Hard Knocks

In the locker room we unhooked our bras, hoping
shower steam kept us invisible,
but our souls showed, our prepubescent fuzz.
Stockings hung from shower rods like biblical snakes.
Who would learn first? we wondered, and drew breasts
in goofy loops until Sister Angelica banged

her ruler, and we printed the same confession
a hundred times, her shadow crossing
our spiral notebooks, her eyes like old
spiders. Ginnie learned and got a heart-shaped
locket, then a shotgun wedding ring.
Heather gave birth so often she forgot,
she said, what caused it. Becky's womb was lost
in an abortionist's garage. We said good-bye

in the Immaculate Conception parking lot.
Still, nuns click their beads in memory of us,
how we strolled, arms linked, singing,
into the world of women where all deaths begin.

Courage

This much is clear: you have to be alone
with grief, to walk each squeaky floorboard
by yourself, to puzzle out what's brought
that tightness to your throat, that salt,
this pouring forth. There is no one you can call,
no number. You have to be alone with this.
And the feathered dancers who distracted you,
the spinning fans, the cinnamon flavor of apples,
the cigarettes you smoked—these will do no good.
The songs will make it worse. You have
to be alone. Someone you loved is gone,
not dead, but step by step away from you,
on purpose, no accident, nothing misunderstood.
The door was pulled tight, the one

of many doors you face in this corridor,
your life, and not one will open,
suddenly framing by a backlit friend.
You have to take this bag of grief,
each little betrayal and pack it small,
roll it like bad wool into a ball,
and with all your strength, your sinew,
your tendons like bow string, place it
on your back, and keep walking,
however slowly, down the hall.

(for Lecia)

Vampire

She starts loving herself.
It's a Catholic nightmare, hair
sprouting on her flesh like clover.
Her lover, embarrassed at public gatherings,
giggles into his wine, explains,
This is some curse.
At dusk he hears a hiss escape from her throat
like steam from a kettle.
The cat disappears. She moves to the basement.
This loving of herself doesn't show up
in mirrors. Everyone warns her,
but she trusts it, melting locks from doors,
passing unnoticed through crowded
supermarkets, a whiff of jasmine.

Incredulous at the growth of her teeth,
her dentist works overtime, first with sandpaper,
then with a small saw.
All the x-rays come back milky.
If her lover had persisted
a little longer, she may have come
to some Christian sense, gone to the seashore
in dark glasses, buttoned her blouse.
He always knew she had it in her.
He seems to grow shorter, pant cuffs
dragging the ground, shoulder blades
growing into a hump
that refuses to be hidden in clothing.
He begins bringing her small animals.

As for the vampire, she remembers nothing
of the innocent life. Can evil know itself?
Her eyes open in her small satin room.
Who could admit loneliness under such conditions?
She has health, good looks, brains,
and a dense little rock of a man who dies
nightly beneath her lips.
There is a point just in the region
of her heart large enough for a hatpin,
a single place that stings
just before she gives herself over
to her own moon.

Vigil

On the night of my homecoming my father slept
a hard sleep, and each breath wet
like weed roots dug in earth.

The moon blurred in the glucose bottle
near his bed. Mother nodded.
A woman wept in the hall.

By the cigarette machine an old man fished coins
from his black click-open purse with such care
I recalled a tender kissing session two blocks

and ten years from there. That first boy was a dope,
or so my father felt, when I arrived flushed,
disheveled, and that summer we rarely spoke.

I was full of sex and Russian novels and the college
we couldn't afford. His war stories scared me,
so he told his secrets to the empty house.

In empty beer bottles he left grocery lists
or chores scrawled in a spidery hand,
written without thought or memory.

A hard sleep. My sister and I played honeymoon
solitaire on the extra bed and watched the clock
and took his vital signs. Morning came.

No peace was made. We washed down aspirin
with bitter coffee, and he poked the plastic
oxygen tent to see where he stopped and we began.

Perspective: Anniversary D-Day

I hauled the army footlocker thunking
up the basement stairs, knelt with my crowbar
as a treasure diver might
who half expects brilliant light or pearl ropes
once the padlock's broken, not forty years
of bank receipts, a sergeant's cap,
some handkerchiefs. A wind gust stirred
so the bundle of war letters appeared

to breathe like an accordion. Lifting each,
I found oblong holes where a censor's razor
sliced out *Italy* or *France*. The studded night
shone through these, as if doors long closed
had blown open.

       My father turned my age
in a mud trench; shoving a pencil stub
across a match-lit page, he wrote, *I'm too old
to start a family now, I guess,* and only asked
for socks and cigarettes, had carved that day
some hometown farm boy's name in the oak
where he'd been shot. *Tell Mr. Fermin
it's a pretty place.* When he climbed dripping
onto a Normandy beach, alert, rifle high,
the sun seemed to float in his eyes.

Tonight I pass my hand before his line of sight
with no response. Italy and France are gone.
On the rest-home TV, gentlemen in wing-tip shoes
speak solemnly, pray, shake hands, then watch
fireworks explode. The screen's odd blue

ignites our wheelchair ring, each nodding head
a death mask carved in ice.
I roll my father back to bed,
where he wobbles the few steps to collapse.
As I lean to kiss him, his mattress tilts
like a raft already broken off, embarking.

For My Children

After high school I ran away to the coast,
slept in a pink Lincoln Continental on blocks
in a deserted lot. By day, I body-surfed
the hollow waves. From orchards I stole fruit,
stuffed it in my tee-shirt like breasts
    I didn't have.

Boredom never troubled me.
At night I traveled everywhere on LSD.
From the warm leather of the dead car
I toured the rolling stars, or the great plains
spotted with buffalo on a beer can, the nearby
    sea rushing like a train,

earth turning beneath my seat like a carpet
yanked by some giant hand. Once I saw
my entire history in an avocado seed,
a quick replay of all my dawns,
until I stared, breathless, at the green pulp
    in my cupped palms,

eyes like black moons from every bad trip
you ever heard. Next day I called my mom.
I spent my mayonnaise jar of cash, saved
for a Mexican holiday, on my ticket home,
then college, then this respectable job
    with my name

embossed on creamy cards, my mail
arriving every day. I hardly budge.
This story isn't meant to warn: no shark
ever circled me, nor did local cops
plot my arrest for drugs or vagrancy.
        And don't fear

aging, stalling in your tracks,
a locked engine, churning in sand.
You're blessed, will remain,
for a time, unborn, without a past,
ignorant of change. This time is false
        and will not last.

2

Diogenes Goes to Town

When I first came to the city
it was hard. Even while I still walked on two legs,
carried correct coins for the bus,
my jokes fell flat, and people laughed
at the bones and roses
embroidered on my ties.
In the bar there was always a snicker
floating over from the next booth
like a shadow unattached to human flesh.
It was as though I lived in a jar
and these shadows, like gnats,
peppered out the sun. I threw away my keys;
I thought it right to live outside.
I knotted my tie around the branches of the yew tree
and *the bones!* the roses never flew so free.
Me! Me! I shouted and no longer gazed at the sky,
expecting some helicopter to lower down a noose.

Lipstick

It's Paris where I use a cigarette
for my night light, a guidebook
to illuminate my mouth:
Bong jewr, Mong sewr
Bare leetz. Travel should be easy,
but all night I've untangled alleys.
When I pucker into my compact, I see
a woman stranded under fat
white lilac trees, and the sky of Paris
is threaded with champagne corks,
shot off balconies like messages
that'll never be caught. I study the map.
I try to imagine the trail of white smoke
my jet must have left behind,
like the wet smear of my tongue
licking closed this envelope.
Some people never learn
how to make a good impression, and my lips
leave two red wings on the back of an aerogram.
Inside it says, "I'm gone;
eat your heart out."
It's Paris makes me speak
this strange language.
I strike a match on the zipper of my jeans
to check a street sign.
It's the *Roo of Burdens*,
and I shake the whole world
dark again.

The Pursuit of Heaven: Sex and the Buddha

1.

She's lost the matchbook from the French hotel where she
explored the positions of the *Kamasutra*, and the map
of India, which he unfolded across her knees,
and which resembled an origami bird. He flew
into himself. He flew like the sparrow
in the print above the bed. In the Himalayas.
In a single stroke of ink with the Buddha
reaching to adjust the stars. She opened her kimono,
and his path was so true he didn't even blink,
but brushed over her like an angel. Eyes
distant, as though her nipples were snowy peaks.

2.

Where he lives now there are no women, only acres
of yellow blossoms, a river, and some mountaintops.
Two stories are sung to him:
a man who arranged the history of the world
in an ebony bowl, with a few grains of rice;
a whore so weary of men
admiring her eyes, she plucked them out,
and it rained gold coins. This pleases him—
wisdom ticking through the clouds, the world
rocking on a stalk of rice.
He shaves his head and sends her a telegram.
    Little Bodhisattva   stop
    The earrings are for dancing   stop
    I've developed new interests   stop

3.
Tonight the stars fall over Paris
like spots on dice tossed years ago.
When she sees them, reflected in the Seine,
it's as asterisks referring to goose flesh
that once rose across her skin. She plops down.
Mister Buddha, she prays
with her penknife in the park bench,
screw the stars in hard tonight,
and the fat concierge who flips a franc into the air
smiles from his window to see her so intense.
At night he studies her through the keyhole.
She studies death, how predictable it is,
as if she can fold the wings of her kimono
and sleep alone, assuming the position she held before
    birth.
Assuming nothing and that nothing hurts.

The Last Paris Poem

The dream we had was Paris, and it was the sweetest lie
I ever heard. *Grace*, you said, and there were swans
feeding on bread you tossed from our taxi window. *Lilac*,
and from the stirrup of your hands, I balanced to tear
branches. *Angel*, and we slung cameras around our necks
like tourists in paradise who can only love
from a distance. This is a snapshot of you
taking a snapshot of me taking a snapshot.
This is Minneapolis, where we breathe snow
in the dark bubble of the car,
where all that remains of *Lilac*
is the fear of falling,
which is the first truth.

Last night I fell asleep with my face on the typewriter.
The keys marked my cheek.
So at dawn I stood at the mirror
to try to read myself like a page of braille.
I don't know who you are or how we once dreamt
of Paris. I watched the perfume-maker squash
a thousand blossoms into his tiny vial. I imagine
your coins still plunk on his glass counter: Grace, Lilac,
Angel, we paid dearly. I rushed at swans with arms wide
until they rose in one graceful heap.
Like the handkerchief I lift as you drive away,
the snowflake I dot behind my ear.
This is a snapshot washed black by the airport x-ray.
It waves good-bye.

My New Diet

A guy in the bar where I drink every night
told me a great lie about pigmies—how they eat

just once a year, when the rains come, and then
it's anything in sight. It was a wet night,

so we drank to the pigmies on their hunt, lifted mugs
to a speared boar dancing in jungle sun,

a happy story ending with a belch, the village
asleep beneath palms and then the waitress

tipping the stools up on the bar. Some nights
you have to take what you hear for fact.

Some nights you have to believe a man just because
he needs to be believed. I swung open the door

to my taxi and took him home. I slithered out
of my black dress like a python while the rain

banged its brains out on the window—the ritual thump
of zebra drums, until the world turned black and white.

No photographs were taken, but I felt captured
when I woke alone at dawn. I put my finger down my
    throat

to return everything false I ever swallowed,
return to the pure feeling I had as a girl,

thumbing through *National Geographic* on Sunday
    morning,
hungry for another place and dying to make something

of myself, however small.

(for Suzanne)

Insomnia

The sheet that covers my head is streaked with roses,
it'll take all night to count them all: each fist,
kiss mark, knot in red rope recurs without surprise
or intrigue, and the boredom of my mistakes is the same.
    When I was twenty

I lifted my breasts with lace and chicken wire.
I found a man who lacked intelligence, but who
unhooked me from behind. My silk stockings
slung across a chair, his cadillac fingers and . . . that was
    long ago. He lived with me

yet I managed to live alone like the sailor I dreamt
at night, who whooped around the sea and then
washed up. I heard a typhoon nearing in his snore.
And now I am alone, not as in marriage, but like
    this page in a magazine:

a palm tree sways above some blue area of the globe.
A man and woman hoist a great, wet sail,
which represents the inability of men and women
to go anywhere together without work and argument.
    I stretch across my raft

at a loss for words, with a bunch of periodicals
for friends. I love in spurts, and the bed upholds
my great need for rest, or just: let the roses float
unmastered, like a woman who gets tired, can't sleep,
    who staggers overboard.

The Distance

I'm sorry we missed each other, but that's the story
two poets write. Your taxi screeched away
as I arrived, your numbered door swung open
to an empty room. I questioned the hotel clerk.
He gave me your envelope,
the box with the single pearl,
strung now with the rest, your gifts,
my abacus of love and hate.

I sat in the hotel bar placing each stone
with its occasion, my birthdays, your infidelities,
the boat trip to Japan where we bought
the Utamaro print that hung above the bed.
A woman diver perched on a slimy rock,
black rope of hair, knife in her teeth.
She'd been down deep, and you admired her.

The print is in a crate somewhere, our names
slid from the mail slot in the apartment complex.
The Oriental couple across the hall, the ones
we thought were spies because they mistook our typing
for gunfire late one night must stare at our old door
through that fishbowl eye, thinking
we're still there, silence
billowing through the rooms like smoky oil.
Quiet killed us after all, what we wrote
but never spoke, what we make appointments
to explain. Why you always dream me in cab's rear view,
screaming the words, *Hello, how are you?* Why

I sit so long in hotel bars, where oysters sleep
on beds of ice. I watch them opened with army knives,
drenched with lemon and salt as if the sea taste
might be tamed. And my waitress
pours my brut champagne, reads *True Romance*,
Confession, whose metaphors are stupid
as this: if the road we traveled was love,
that black typewriter ribbon,
some clumsy thumb keeps striking the return.

Return. I think of your hands in Hong Kong,
dug into a sack of seedy pearls, how I forgave you
again and again, each blue-black midnight
a thin layer on a shell.
The dangle of the rickshaw puller's spine
a familiar question mark, and *sorry*
in the slap, slap of his thongs
as he dragged us down the narrowing street.

Old Mistakes

What is this fascination with history, this
    eagerness to return to what's been
done. I wake with a start on your pillow
    and hear in your familiar breath

the sound of shovels in wet earth.
No one digging into this dream
could guess how far back our fingers reach
    when we touch, which is to say:

how deeply we bury each other.

(after Marina Tsvetayeva)

Every Morning

The woman whose lover is away steals through the alley
snipping flowers from neighbors' yards:
honeysuckle, iris, an occasional lucky rose.
The lover lives with his wife or has a job
in another city, something that keeps them apart.
While most couples wake to warm breathing,
she hears the clip of metal scissors,
stems and leaves dropping into her paper bag
with a tapping like fingernails on a wooden table
or brief rain. Sometimes the alley is still dark,
and she peers into a window—two people
tangled in sheets. For a moment
she feels her lover's arm on her shoulder,
simple as brown thread on a spool, as if
he were walking her to the bus stop or taxi stand.
She shivers with the memory. Then the fact
of his absence slips over her, and once more
he's torn away. Birds chatter. Neighbors take in milk.
And the alley lined with gardens,
which briefly filled her heart with possibility,
seems like an endless black road she must trudge
day after day with her burden of flowers
and her wild ideas of arrangement.

Diogenes Tries to Forget

It's one of those days when everything's half-off,
half-on. My shirt, for example, which I notice
is buttoned wrong while staring in the diner window.
I think I want a slice of pecan pie, some life
sweeter than this, like my childhood in Texas.
There's no pie today, just you,
by accident again, bent over your coffee
like the "V" the geese fly south.

It's a fall day. Because we're melancholy
we kick leaves, pick up rocks to consider
tossing them at dogs. *I only breathe with one lung
since you've gone*, you say. And I love you
with one hemisphere of my brain,
the dumb one, which forgets.

Exile's Letter

Dearest dear, from far away I write
wanting to shape a boat
from these white leaves of paper,
a frail shell, something to reach you.

I woke this morning foggy,
everything phantom, pearl mist
tumbled down the mountain
over sleeping columbine and spruce.

I trudged through snow to the mailbox.
No letter from you. My fingers burned
on ice metal. I wanted to crawl inside,
to chalk blue horses on the walls,
or to pull a chair dead center, to have
a serious talk with my emptiness.

Our years together barely fill one hand,
yet what I thought my strongest
characteristics—restraint, cruelty,
a blind attention to the self—are gone. How

can I defeat my enemies? Even now
their hounds test the wind for this place,
howling, howling in my skull, in the small
bones of my inner ear reserved for your words.

Predictions

Soon you will vanish into thin air.
I know this the way the man in my neighborhood
knew tornadoes. Sometimes when the sky was spotless
   blue,
the fillings in his teeth would sting,
then a black funnel cloud would rise and drop,
tearing up the town's whole future—
pigs, chickens, fields of rice. Was he not blessed
to know death in such good weather? Even now

after supper on this sunny deck
I can't enjoy the sea. It doesn't matter
that your shirt is bleached white
or that your neck smells of mint shaving cream,
clean and hopeful as next year. I can only grieve
for empty lobster shells split on the blue plate,
feeling this day give way to other days, how sad
the triangle of your back would be
if you turned to walk away.
This is the curse of drawing inward, and this
is how to die alone, by focusing on doubt
till it becomes a turbulent center in the skull,
a giant straw through which everything is sucked
like my mouth forming an "o"
through which all kisses disappear.

A Kind of Clarity

In the first slop blizzard of the season, the sky
turns blue-dark by four o'clock, and in the square
we've bought books, raisins for baking,
and there I'm suddenly precious to you.
But because it's Christmas, because a boy
zigzags on ice skates across the pond, because
we are aging and his screams are a lesson in adult
disappointment, you turn from me, drop my arm.
You watch your retired professor at the chestnut cart.
For him, Christmas is a cafeteria meal, eaten alone;
how you envy his bachelor apartment, his television's
    blue
forgiving eye, and now there are chestnuts in your mind.
Small stones of doubt, steaming in a white paper bag
in the raveled pocket you've imagined for yourself.

Tonight you'll slump in the red leather chair
reading Flaubert's letters, sad tales of long
labor and loss, written to a poet the world
forgot. I will be edited from your thoughts
like an embarrassing diary page, and you'll nod off,
warm with your secrets, which are a kind of clarity.
Flaubert knew that, knew that the heart
is an encyclopedia of longing, a jeweled book
that best describes what's missing or never was.
Across town the old man will close his Bible, one night
closer to death, and if you stepped into his life
briefly today, I will enter your hidden self,
crack the rough shell you've fashioned
from which a blade of warm starlight escapes,
a clue that something beautiful can be born.

3

Witnessing My Father's Will

I tell the only truth I know:
that I'm helpless and sorry you're dying,
that this planet will weigh no less when you
are ash. I will continue speaking steadily,
wearing black, whatever is necessary,
and if, as Buddha says, life and death are illusory,
I will be fooled and suffer your absence,
and somewhere you'll always be
rising from your oxygen tent, a modern Lazarus,
or snapping open a Lone Star beer,
or simply, too tired to talk, scraping mud
from your black work boots onto the porch.
And if, as Wittgenstein thinks, problems are grammatical,
I confess I find no syntax to pull
nails from a coffin, no exclamation
to shock words back into your brain,
or to electrify your numb legs into a walk.
In college I was taught there's nobility
in perseverance, and so crown you king
because you stare without blinking at the doctor's
wristwatch as he thumps your heart,
because your arms are ghostly bone.
And if such thoughts sap your strength,
I'll inherit your seventy years
of silence, accepting your theory
that theories are garbage, thinking in shrugs.

Diogenes Consoles a Friend

You can make a friend of grief,
paint its face white, offer it
a kimono to wear, a cup of tea.
When all your real friends are gone
you can walk through the woods with it,
burying little jars
stuffed with their memories—
photo-booth snapshots, some jewels,
until real life grows so vague
your landlord thinks
you're crazy. Grief expects this
and invents funny insults about
your landlord's wife and the possibility
of love. You may decide the events
of your day—writing, bathing,
cashing checks—were hobbies
anyway, so you forget them
to think of your own death
more purely. You lie around a lot.
An old friend drops by unexpectedly,
saying you're pale, get dressed,
have a beer. But you're
too smart for that. You admire anyone
simply for not being you. Grief
has taken off its mask.
Standing behind you, it is smoke
or cologne or ghost; it now steps
into your sleeping arms like sleeves,
blinking for you, scrambling your brains.

(for Bill Knott)

Diogenes the Bartender Closes Up

Thank God for the bankrupt drunk with the gold
American Express. He bought my gin.
He understood my thoughts, punched the saddest
numbers on the jukebox.
His divorce will join the myths
in my best Iliad.
And bless the maintenance man, that holy ghost,
a blue-eyed vet who mops
the four corners of my world, a ring of keys
that can open any door
singing from his belt. I feel locked up.
I'm some rigmarole
they hired cheap. I know fine art, the alphabet.
I don't know why the screws
tighten in our lives, or how to move a single
inch beyond myself.

(for David St. John)

Moving Days

Folding the old Monopoly board
I straighten the piss-yellow $500 bills.
If this were real . . . we thought as kids.

That sense of possibility is gone
though artifacts remain: the dirty string
that knotted charms—flat iron, silver shoe,

the choo-choo I might have ridden
anywhere. These rest in a junkyard sofa
or twinkle in the belly of the fish

we tilted down the toilet bowl.
And the great chain of command
yanks another notch, and I pack

this year's books for next year's
crackerbox, where I'll stand at the door,
glancing down the green road.

Like the woman I dreamed
on the step of my sturdy Boardwalk house
I'll kiss my hopeful pin-striped man

and listen for the thunder of the dice.

Night Answering Service

I slept there on a roll-out cot school nights,
the switchboard periodically buzzing me awake,
so I'd plug my headset into a red-lit slot
where a stranger screamed for a doctor's help.
  I broke a sweat

with death so close. Unplugging the phone line,
I'd hear the ambulance's lullaby.
Nightmares trailed each episode. Pulses and cries
I couldn't decode flooded the strange network
  of corridors in my head

till I sat up, peered hard, raised the blinds:
The boiling flames from oil-refinery towers
and chemical plants lit the walls. The graveyard
shift whistle blew, and I'd picture my father
  clocking out. Each day

he stopped by my job at purple dusk to deliver
my steamy supper plate wrapped in foil.
How could I know death would unlace his boots,
thread a circuit in the blue signals of his brain
  and whittle out his core

to leave this sad figure curled in a nursing home.
He twists with great tortoise effort to press lips
to the milk straw I hold. Long after the carton's empty
and he's dozed off, I hesitate to pull it free, the straw
  a contact point, a cord

in the multicolored web that links us, ties us down.

Beyond Freedom and Dignity

1. The Operations
Despite your gentleness with the syringe, the mice
die on the table. Their tails stiffen like pencils
in your coat. While they lived, they dreamt, and needles
scribbled their stories onto a pale blue grid.
It convinced you: the mind is a palpable thing.
And you're right. With a pair of tweezers you can hold
the part that really counts. The rest for luck, the skull
strung with nerves, rivers to let the world rush in.

2. The Sensory-Deprivation Experiments
Once you told me about a scientist who wrapped a man
in cotton and took away his feelings, or tried to,
by lowering him into a warm swimming pool.
But behind black goggles he still saw light.
You remember this when you're blind with fatigue.
Strolling the rows of cages in the lab,
you realize there's no point
in pressing your thumbs to your eyelids.
Some pearl of torture stays alive.
It's what you're diving for down the black tunnel
of the microscope. You remove your spectacles
and believe your heart, hooked to a screen,
would produce a long white line.

3. *Morning*
If this were the line of reason you followed
with your scalpel—one end of a tiny spine
to the other—the mouse sleeping in your cupped palm
would sleep forever and be deprived. Your breath
is warm as you lean over him.
The electrodes you planted in his brain
tell him he's happy. His eyelids tremble with pleasure.
You make a check on the chart.
How manageable dreams are
when shrunk to size and held dear
one square inch at a time. It's nearly dawn
when you unbutton your coat, switch off
the last light. The mice glow in their cages
like plucked chrysanthemums. Their pupils,
as they dilate, seem to breathe.

(for Walt Mink)

Diogenes Passes the Time

The days, yellow-hot and dull,
flip on the calendar's spiral whose twist
I follow idly, with little interest.
Staring out the window: yard and neighbors.
I look for the first time on this age: how
we've changed, predictably, believing
too much. That's the bourgeois curse.
Words that befuddled me as a child—
martini, mortgage due—are spoken to me daily
and resound with truth.

If I trust the old beliefs, and slowly,
inch by inch, crawl exactly where I'm told,
what sad nights I'll cradle in my lap.
I fail to prevent this somewhat. I join
the other adults, breathing my life
insurance like a drug. I sound ridiculous
at political rallies where the only beef
is the six ounces on each idiot's plate.
Not that I mean to joke. Hello,
my age, I am resigned to you.

(for Robert Long)

Letter from an Airplane

Years ago I flew away from you.
I had faith. It flickers now like a star.
"Where are you?" you ask on a Christmas card.

In seat 3D, in midnight air,
wearing a fourteen-carat sacred heart,
your gift the year I got remote;
and the urge to be holy, to write the truth,
becomes a joke: I am Mary
who gives birth to deep regret
in airplanes, on postcards signed Les Ismore.
Is it enough? The stars still plastered to the glass.
I drink too much; I'm scared I've gone too far.
If I bail out now over this small Montana town
where you live with your dumb wife, would you rush
    out?
Or buckle yourself in, click out the light,
regard each parachute as a giant flake of snow,
some natural mistake.
Like belief in God, in love,
how I thought I could live alone.

Everything looks up, I write as snow drifts down.
I thought we'd both be dead by now.
On the wing a blue light dims.
Wheels scrape ground, and I could weep ice cubes
for all the thoughts that count. Please think
we're angels hung on separate trees,
dangling in our dark selves, houses
lit by candles, drippy stars.

Home During a Tropical Snowstorm
I Feed My Father Lunch

It angers me: the cold snap and freak ice storm
that's wrecked my yearly pilgrimage home.
Coming far from my northern province, I miss
the perfume of the cape jasmine,
and I want to smash the hard mush of tomatoes
in paint cans on the porch against the white house
and axe the crackling trees.
Such burden on the earth: no electricity,
no phone, just this glass coat that prevents
my really seeing, really feeling anything—
iced magnolia blossoms, bananas sagging
like gold ingots from the weight.

It's like the repression my father practiced,
who draped a dishtowel on his shaving mirror
against vanity, his tough Indian face
too beautiful. *What you can't see*
won't hurt, he said, and meant it
modestly and worked in every weather—
tropical heat waves, hurricanes.
He trusted the natural order of things,
which means he rests this day
on a soiled bed sheet,
while an inch-deep sore carves itself
into his butt. And it takes an infinity
to spoon beef stew into his vacant face.
Vanity aside, you might have studied
yourself, Father, whose portrait
on the empty spoon's silver I resemble:
long-faced, mouth stretched into a yowl.

***

When he gasps and chokes blue on the fibrous meat,
a full space bar strikes in my chest as I review
the oath I made the doctor take
not to jolt his heart or ever to notch
his windpipe for an automatic lung.
And that night I unwrapped the army pistol
from his tangled socks and underwear,
cleaned it with mechanical oil he kept
and sat on the porch weighing
its male bulk and simplicity:
the crossed hairs like a plus sign
on the frozen orange moon,
but though glands in my throat
soured with the wish,
I could not invite his death.
And when he choked
I pried the leather jaw open,
poked my finger past the slick gums
to scoop an air passage
till he bit down hard and glared,
an animal dignity glowing
in those bird-black eyes,
which carried me past pity
for once, for once
all this terror twisting into joy.

Report

All winter I stared at my hands.
Sometimes I made a telescope of them
through which I viewed the world.

There was a window where a still life
of waves said nothing of my future but
again, again. There was a man

whose hunger was a hard red jewel.
Everything we felt we had to test
like ants who extend antennae to probe

the earth, a crumb, the feelers
of a stranger ant discovered in some dark
tunnel. Such curiosity

disappoints at the end of love stories,
though tenderness endures. That's the secret,
tenderness: one tiny message drawn by a fingernail

on the palm of someone sleeping.

(for Michael)

Note: Diogenes was the first Cynic. The speaker of the Diogenes poem is a distant, contemporary cousin. *(See pages 23, 35, 42, 43, and 48.)*